Toys
around the
World

Brian Moses

All around the world, children love to play with toys.

The children may dress in different ways. They may speak in different ways.

But they can't do without toys.

Don't you agree?

Children in China like to play with toy tigers like these. Toy tigers have been popular in China for a long time. They are traditional toys.

These are traditional Russian toys. The dolls fit into each other one by one. Russian children like to fit the dolls into each other. They start with the very little one.

Do you like traditional toys?

3

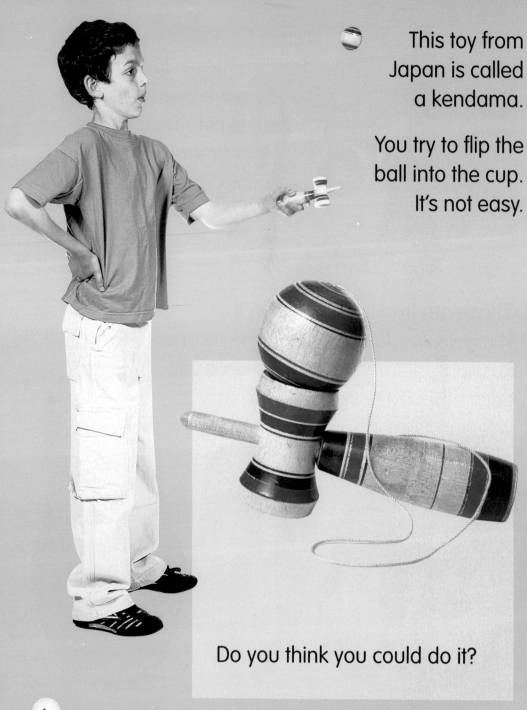

This toy from Japan is called a kendama.

You try to flip the ball into the cup. It's not easy.

Do you think you could do it?

Many children like to play with teddy bears.

This is a bear made in the United States. It is made from a soft, furry material. It has felt pads for hands and feet. Can you see what the eyes are made of?

Do you have a teddy bear?

Does it help you get to sleep at night?

In this photograph
a boy is selling toys
made from wire.

The toys have
moving parts.
They are popular in Botswana, in Africa.

Have you seen toys like this before?

This is a toy plane from Bolivia. It is made of straw.

Wooden dolls are traditional toys in Mexico. These wooden dolls are made by hand.

Do you think the straw plane from Bolivia would last a long time?

Do you think the wooden dolls made in Mexico would last a long time?

Children love toys. Toys are important to children all over the world.

How would you feel if you didn't have toys?

Could you imagine a world without toys?